I Wonder
Why Fish Don't Drown

· · · · · · · · · · · · · · · · · ·

and other neat facts about underwater
animals

By Annabelle Donati
Illustrated by David Schulz

A GOLDEN BOOK • NEW YORK
Western Publishing Company, Inc., Racine, Wisconsin 53404

Produced by Graymont Enterprises, Inc., Norfolk, Connecticut
Producer: *Ruth Lerner Perle*
Design: *Michele Italiano-Perla*
Editorial consultant: *Jacques Padawer, Ph.D.*, Albert Einstein College of Medicine, New York

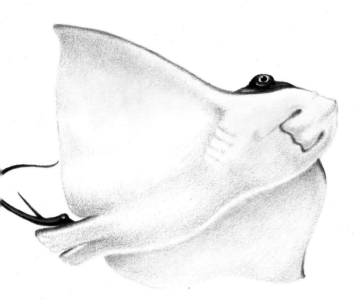

Contents

What does it take to be a fish?

The most amazing kinds of animals make their homes in water. They come in every imaginable shape and size, and in every color of the rainbow. Some can move as fast as sixty miles an hour, others hardly move at all. Some live at the bottom of the salty sea, some in freshwater ponds and rivers. But not all sea animals are fish.

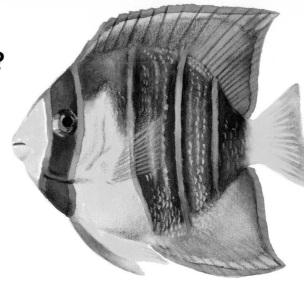

Why are fish so slimy?

Most fish have a slippery covering over their bodies to help them move smoothly through the water and also to protect them from infections.

Do fish ever sleep?

Fish have no eyelids, so they can't close their eyes. But most do sleep—usually behind rocks or seaweed. Some, like the tuna and the shark, rarely stop swimming.

Most fish have:

A boat-shaped body

Tapered at both ends, its streamlined shape helps a fish move smoothly through the water. Some fish, like sea horses and eels, do not have tapered bodies.

Gills

Instead of lungs, fish have gills. These are organs that take oxygen out of the water.

Fins

Fish don't have legs. They use fins to steer them through the water.

Scales

Most fish have layers of transparent flat disks called scales covering their body.

Bones

Most fish are *vertebrates*. They have a movable backbone as part of the hard, bony skeleton inside their body.

"Cold" blood

A fish's body temperature is the same as the temperature of the water in which it swims.

Are all animals that live under the water fish?

There are other creatures that live under the water, but they belong to different groups of animals. They are not vertebrates. They do not have fins or scales. They do not have a bony skeleton or a backbone. They are *invertebrates,* such as jellyfish, squids, crabs sponges, clams, and starfish.

Even though all these invertebrate creatures are so different, one thing about them is the same: They all live in water and never have to come up for air.

Amazing
but TRUE

Fish never stop growing. The older they get, the bigger they grow. You can tell the age of a fish by counting the number of rings on its scales.

Why don't fish drown?

All animals need oxygen to live. Animals that live on land get their oxygen from the air they breathe. They *inhale* the air through their mouth or nose. Then the air goes to their lungs. The lungs take the oxygen out of the air, which is breathed out again, or *exhaled*, through the mouth or nose. Fish get their oxygen from water. The fish's gills must do the job of lungs.

A land animal, such as a cow, bird, or elephant, can get oxygen only if it breathes air. If it remained underwater, it would suffocate and drown because of a lack of oxygen. A fish can get oxygen only from water. If it remained out of the water, it would suffocate and die of a lack of oxygen. A fish would "drown" in the air.

6

How do fish keep from sinking?

Many fish have an inflatable *swim bladder* in their body. A little like a balloon or tube, the bladder helps the fish float in the water. A fish can control the amount of air it has in its swim bladder. The more it inflates its bladder, the more support it has.

Fish that don't have a swim bladder cannot float. If these fish stop moving forward, they sink.

How do gills work?

A fish gulps water in through its mouth. The water then streams over its gills, which take the oxygen out of the water. Then the water goes back out through openings at the sides of the fish's head.

Amazing *but* TRUE

Some fish also use their bladder as an eardrum to pick up sounds. Others use it to amplify their own sounds.

7

Can a crab jump out of its skin?

Crabs don't actually jump out of their skins, but they do wriggle out when they need to grow bigger. Crabs and their cousins, lobsters and shrimps, have no bones. Instead, their bodies are covered with a hard shell that supports and protects their soft insides. The shell is both a crab's skin and its skeleton, called an *exoskeleton*.

As the crab's body grows, its shell gets too small. When the shell splits, the crab crawls out—this is called *molting*. Now the crab has only a soft skin covering its body.

As soon as it has molted, the crab drinks a lot of water so that its body swells up before its new soft skin hardens into a shell.

How does a crab see where it is going?

A crab has two sets of feelers, or *antennae*, extending from its head. These antennae have two thin stalks with knoblike eyes at their tips. The crab can move these stalks so it can see in any direction.

Because its eyes are placed above its head, the crab can bury itself in the sand and still see what's going on around it.

Crab shells are full of calcium and other nourishment, so most crabs make a meal of their discarded armor.

8

How do crabs move from place to place?

Like their land relatives—spiders—crabs have four pairs of jointed legs. Some crabs have one pair of legs shaped like paddles, which they use to push themselves along in the water.

Why do crabs have claws?

The crab uses its two clawlike front legs for tearing food into bits.

The male fiddler crab has one very large, brightly colored claw. He holds this claw up and waves it to attract females. He uses the other, smaller claw like a knife to scrape food off rocks.

When a crab loses a claw, another one grows in its place.

Tell Me More

The hermit crab has no hard exoskeleton, so it looks for any empty shell and crawls into it for protection. When its body grows too big for its borrowed "apartment," the hermit crab finds a bigger shell and moves in.

Why does a shark have so many teeth?

Sharks are the sea's greatest *predators*. That means they hunt and eat live fish and other sea creatures, and a few may attack people. They have razor-sharp teeth—and lots of them—to get all the food they need. In fact, sharks have an endless supply of teeth. New teeth are always growing near the back of the shark's jaw. When a tooth is lost, worn out, or broken, a new one moves slowly forward to replace it.

The whale shark is the largest fish in the sea. It has three thousand teeth. But its teeth are very small. It feeds only on tiny shrimps, small fish, and a soupy mixture of tiny plants and animals called *plankton*.

What is sharkskin?

Instead of regular scales, sharks have tiny toothlike points sticking out of their skin. Sharkskin is so rough that it was once used by carpenters to smooth and polish wood.

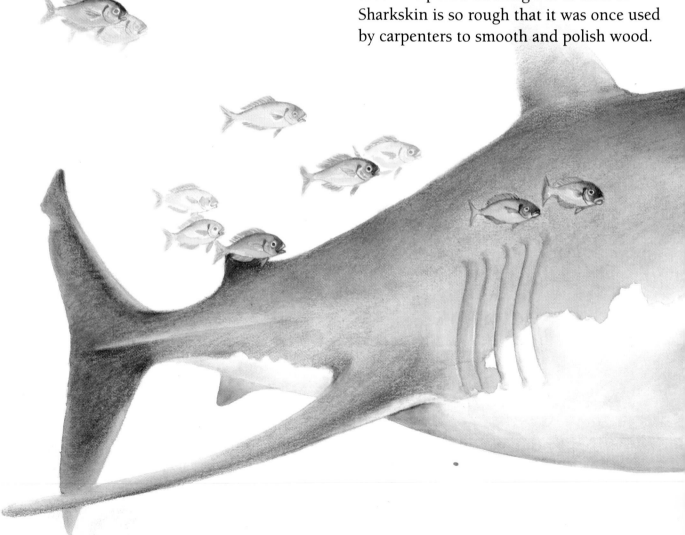

Are all sharks dangerous?

There are more than two hundred fifty kinds of sharks in the sea. About twenty-five kinds are dangerous to human beings. They include the hammerhead, tiger, and mako. But the most dangerous man-eating shark is the white shark, also called the great white shark. It can eat large sea animals in one bite.

Blue sharks are called the wolves of the sea because they travel in packs. They are vicious sharks that will even eat members of their own family.

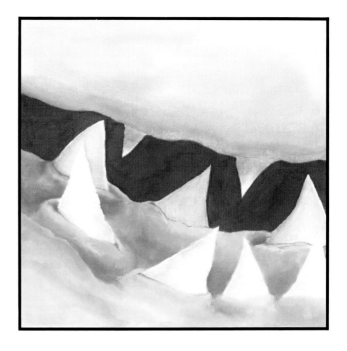

What do shark teeth look like?

Some sharks have teeth that are shaped like triangles; other sharks have teeth that are dagger-shaped.

How does a shark eat its prey?

If the shark catches a smaller fish, it just gulps it down whole. But if it catches a big fish like a tuna, the shark clamps its teeth on its victim's body and cuts it into pieces by shaking it from side to side.

How big is a shark?

Some sharks are as big as a bus, others are only a foot long. The dwarf shark is the smallest—about the size of your hand.

Tell Me More

Sharks may have strong muscles and big teeth, but they have small brains. Dolphins, which are mammals, are not as strong as sharks, but they are much smarter and can usually find ways to escape from sharks by outwitting them. Sometimes they lead sharks on a merry chase until the sharks are so tired that they give up.

Why does the catfish have whiskers?

Catfish have long, threadlike feelers around the mouth that look like cats' whiskers. These feelers have taste buds that help catfish find food in muddy water and guide their way along the dark bottom of a pond.

How do catfish protect themselves?

Catfish have sharp spines in their fins. These spines stick into any creature that handles or tries to swallow the catfish.

Amazing *but* TRUE

Some types of catfish can travel over land from pond to pond, using their front fins to push themselves along the ground. When out of the water, they release a slimy substance that covers their bodies and keeps them moist. In addition to their gills, these catfish have air bladders that they use like lungs when they are on land.

Do flying fish have wings?

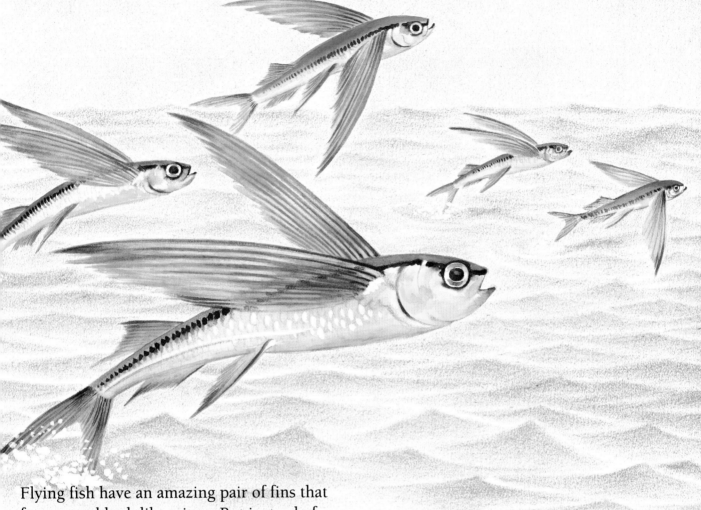

Flying fish have an amazing pair of fins that fan out and look like wings. But instead of flapping them as a bird does, these fish stretch out their fins and glide.

How do flying fish manage to fly?

When flying fish are swimming, they fold their fins against their bodies and swim like any other fish in the sea. But when they want to fly, they turn upward and shoot out of the water. Then they spread their long fins and glide through the air.

Why do flying fish fly?

Most predators are faster swimmers than flying fish and could easily catch them if it weren't for their unusual escape route—up and away into the air.

Tell Me More

The South American hatchetfish is the only fish that can actually flap its winglike fins and fly like a bird. It can fly in the air for a few feet, but then must return to the water for oxygen.

Amazing but TRUE

Some fish, like batfish and gurnard, live at the bottom of the ocean. They use their fins for walking along the ocean floor.

13

Why do flounders have both eyes on one side?

Flounders are flat fish that look like swimming pancakes. They swim on their side along the ocean floor with both eyes facing up on the same side of their head. But flounders are not born swimming on their side. When they hatch, they swim upright near the sea's surface.

As the flounder grows, an amazing—almost magical—change takes place. The flounder's body flattens and turns so that it lies on its side. Usually its right side becomes its top side, and its left side becomes its underside. In this position the flounder would have one eye facing up and the other facing the bottom. Therefore, as the fish flattens, its left eye moves over its head and next to its right eye so that both eyes end up on the top side. The flounder then lies on the sandy bottom, using both eyes to look for food that might be swimming above.

Tell Me More

It is often hard to detect a flounder, even when it is in plain sight. That's because the flounder's top side always blends in with its background. This is called *camouflage*.

Most flounders look like the gravel or sandy seafloor on which they lie. If they move to a different place, they change color to match their new surroundings. They turn a light tan when they are on light sandy ground, and dark gray or black against dark stones or seaweed.

In a camouflage test, flounders were put against a black-and-white-checkered background to see what would happen to their colors. To everyone's amazement, the fish developed a light and dark pattern to match.

Can sea horses gallop?

No, a sea horse cannot gallop because it isn't a horse at all. The sea horse is one of the strangest fish in the sea. It has a head shaped like a pony's and a tail that looks like a snake. Instead of scales, its body is covered with hard, thorny plates. Unlike other fish, it moves through the water with its head up and its tail down. When it wants to rest, it curls its tail around some seaweed to stop itself from floating away.

What do sea horses eat?

Sea horses eat only living things, such as fish eggs, small sea creatures, or tiny plants. When they find a tasty morsel, they just suck it into their long, tubelike mouth.

Bringing up baby

It is not the mother but the father sea horse that gives birth to baby sea horses. The female lays her eggs in the sand. The male then picks them up and places them inside a pouch, or pocket, that he has in front of his belly. He then carries the eggs in his pouch until they hatch. After the babies hatch, they live in their father's pocket until they are strong enough to swim off by themselves. Sometimes the eggs of several females will be taken into a male's pouch. Scientists have found males carrying as many as two hundred eggs!

Australian cousin

The leafy sea dragon is an Australian sea horse. Its irregular skin flaps look like floating seaweed, so it blends into its surroundings and can hardly be seen.

16

The sea horse moves its back fin so fast that it looks like a little spinning pinwheel.

Why does a sponge have holes?

A sponge's holes are a network of hollow tubes that distribute food and water through the sponge's body.

Sponges are strange creatures. They have no head, mouth, eyes, feelers, bones, heart, lungs, or brain. They have no sense organs, and they don't react to the loudest sound or the roughest touch. In fact, a sponge is not a single animal. It is really a colony of thousands of tiny animal organisms living together in a mass.

Where do sponges live?

Most sponges live in shallow seawater, where they are anchored to rocks or other solid surfaces. They can be green, brown, yellow, red, orange, pink, blue, purple, or white. They can be as tiny as a pea or as large as a deer. They can be shaped like tree branches, balls, pillars, or fans.

How can we tell that sponges are animals?

Sponges are considered animals because of the way they feed. Unlike plants, which can make their own nourishment, sponges must capture their food.

Tell Me More

Some small shrimps and crabs live inside the sponge. As the water streams through the sponge's tubes, these animals take some of the food the sponge doesn't get.

Amazing but TRUE

No matter how many pieces you cut a sponge into, each piece will go on living and growing. If you cut a sponge in two, you'll end up with two live sponges. If you cut it into ten pieces, you'll get ten separate live sponges.

Where do shells come from?

If you've ever walked along the seashore, you've probably seen all kinds of shells lying on the beach. These shells are the empty homes of sea animals called shelled *mollusks*. Some mollusks, like snails, live inside single tunnellike shells that are shaped like cones or coils. These animals are *univalves*. Others, like clams, oysters, scallops, and mussels, have two shells that are connected by a hinge and can open and close like a box. They are called *bivalves*.

How do clams breathe?

Like all living things, clams need oxygen. Since clams bury themselves in the sand, they use their tube-shaped *syphon* like a straw to reach up and suck water past their gills. The gills take oxygen out of the water as it flows by. Mussels and oysters don't have syphons, so they just let the water wash through their shells.

How do bivalves travel?

When a scallop wants to move from place to place, it flaps its shell open and shut to push itself through the water. But most bivalves don't do very much traveling. Many stay in one place most of their lives. Mussels actually anchor themselves to a rock with strong threads. Oysters make a kind of cement to attach themselves to rock or coral.

20

Amazing
but TRUE

How do clams eat?

Clams open and close their shells so that the seawater will flow through their bodies. The seawater brings bits of food with it, which the clam traps.

Shells were once used like money. Each type of shell had a certain value. The more shells people had, the richer they were. Native Americans used quahog shells to make beads. Purple ones were rarer, so they were worth more than white ones.

Tell Me More

As clams grow, their shells grow with them, forming rows of ridges. You can tell how old a clam is by counting these ridges.

21

Do starfish twinkle?

No, starfish don't twinkle. They don't shine at all, but they *do* have rays! These rays are arms arranged in a star pattern around a disk in the middle. Many kinds of starfish live in the deep sea, but others can be found on rocks and in shallow pools near the shore.

Despite their name, starfish are not fish. They don't have scales, fins, or bones. Like their cousins, sea urchins and sand dollars, whose bodies are also rough and crusty, starfish are *echinoderms*.

The top side of the starfish is covered with bumps and thorny spines, and its underside has long grooves running down the arms. Along the side of these grooves are hundreds of tiny tubes, called feet, that act like little suction cups. Starfish use these feet to pull and push their bodies slowly along.

Starfish come in all sizes. The largest of all is the sunflower star. It has more than twenty-six arms! When a starfish loses an arm, another one grows in its place. In fact, a starfish can grow a whole new body from just one arm!

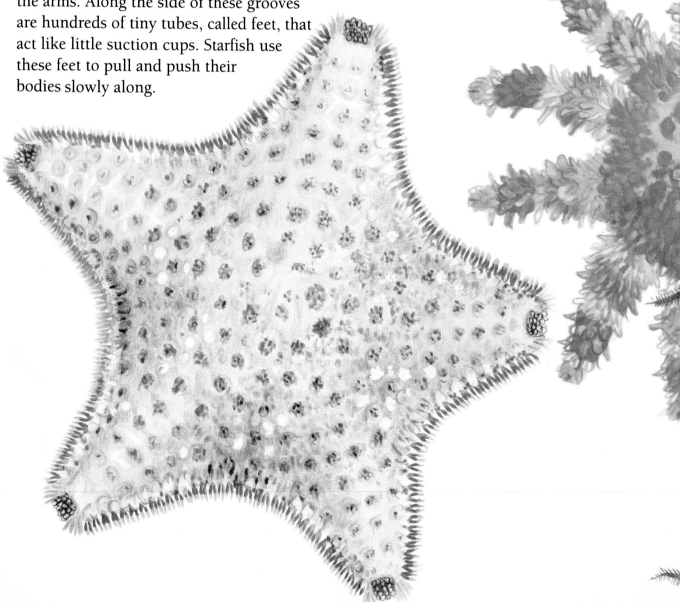

How does a starfish eat?

The starfish's mouth is on its underside—at the middle of its body. It uses its rays to find mussels, oysters, and clams. When a starfish finds a clam, it climbs on top of it, attaches its suction-cup feet, and pulls and pulls until it forces the clam's shell open.

Then the most amazing thing happens. The starfish turns its stomach inside out and brings it out through its mouth. Then the starfish wraps its stomach around the clam and eats the soft meat inside.

Tell Me More

The starfish has an eye at the tip of each of its arms. The eyes can only distinguish light from dark. Each eye is protected by a circle of spines that act like eyelashes.

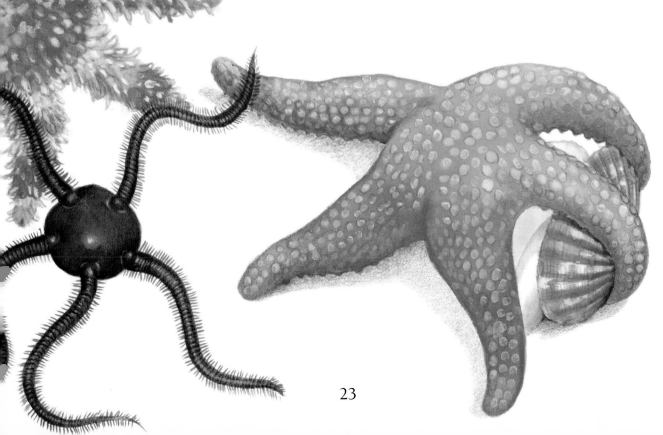

23

How does the pearl get in the oyster?

The pearls people wear around their necks started out as tiny bits of sand or shell that found their way into oyster shells. The oyster's soft body feels uncomfortable with this rough-edged object, so it covers the irritating object with *nacre,* or *mother-of-pearl*, which is the same material as the inside of the oyster's shell. This is the beginning of a pearl. The longer the object stays in the oyster, the more layers of nacre it gets and the larger the pearl becomes.

Pearl farmers make cultured pearls by inserting small shell beads into the oyster's body and letting the oyster do its magic for about three years. Then the pearl is big enough to be made into jewelry. Cultured pearls are produced in Japan, Australia, and Burma, but most of the beads used to start these pearls come from Mississippi River clamshells.

Natural pearls are more valuable than cultured pearls because they are almost solid nacre. Cultured pearls have only a thin layer of nacre over an artificial center.

Amazing *but* TRUE

The largest pearl ever found was about three-quarters of an inch in diameter. That's this size:

Tell Me More

The inside of an abalone shell is lined with nacre. This lining is used for making mother-of-pearl jewelry.

Are eels snakes?

Eels look very much like snakes, but they are a different type of animal. Snakes are reptiles, while eels are fish.

Round-trip passage

Freshwater eels swim from North American and European rivers all the way to a special calm place in the Atlantic Ocean called the Sargasso Sea. There they lay their eggs. These eels know where to go by *instinct*, a behavior they are born with.

When baby eels hatch, they look like tiny transparent leaves. Soon they start their long journey toward the freshwater rivers.

On their way, the tiny glasslike fish grow into little eels, called *elvers*. It can take three years before the young elvers get back to where their parents came from. When the eels are grown and ready to have babies, they make the journey back to the Sargasso Sea, where they were born.

Amazing *but* TRUE

Even though the deep-sea gulper eel has a long, thin body, it can swallow prey twice its size in one big gulp.

A shocking tale

The electric eel has special chemicals along its body. These create a current like that in a battery. Eels use their electric current to defend themselves and to stun—and even electrocute—fish they want to eat.

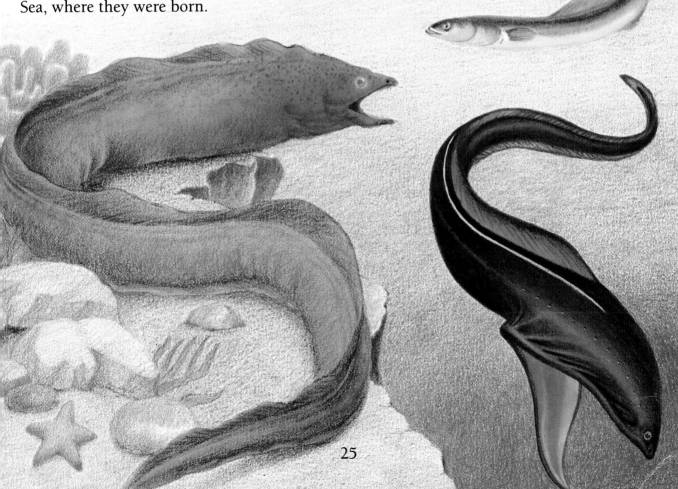

Why does an OCTOPUS squirt ink?

Octopuses and squids cannot swim fast enough to escape danger, so they perform some amazing disappearing acts.

When an octopus is threatened by a predator such as a shark, it releases a cloud of black ink from a special compartment in the lower part of its body. While the confused shark tries to find its way through the inky water, the octopus makes its escape.

How does the octopus move from one place to another?

First the octopus takes water into a space inside its body and closes the opening. Then it forces the water out of its body through a funnellike tube. The force of the water shooting out from behind pushes the octopus forward. You'll get a similar effect when you inflate a balloon and then release it. The force of the air coming out of the balloon shoots it forward. This is also the way a jet plane flies.

Monsters!

Many myths and fairy tales tell about giant man-eating octopuses. This may be partly because octopuses have large heads and bulging eyes. And their jaws are as tough as a parrot's beak.

In fact, octopuses are usually shy animals that live in caves, and even in sunken ships at the bottom of the sea. They come out to catch and eat fish and crabs—not human beings—and then crawl right back into their hiding places.

Tell Me More

Like the clam and the oyster, the octopus is a mollusk, but its head can easily be seen and its fleshy body is not covered by shells. Each of its eight arms is lined with rows of suckers for grabbing and grasping.

Tell Me More

In just minutes an octopus can change its color to match its surroundings so that it becomes very hard to find.

What are jellyfish made of?

Although they look and feel like globs of shimmering jelly, jellyfish are neither jelly nor fish. These strange transparent sea creatures are made almost entirely of water. Most have bodies shaped like an upside-down bowl or an open umbrella, called a *bell,* which has many long tentacles dangling from it.

Tell Me More

Some jellyfish are so small you need a microscope to see them. Others are no bigger than your little finger. But some giants may stretch out to be twelve feet wide. Their tentacles grow a hundred feet long. That's longer than the distance from third base to home plate.

How do jellyfish swim?

Jellyfish can drift with the current and tide, or they can move through the water by squeezing their bell open and shut. This movement forces a stream of water out behind them and pushes their bodies forward.

How do jellyfish catch fish?

A jellyfish can stun a fish or shrimp with poisonous stingers on its tentacles. Or it can use its tentacles like ropes to hold on to its prey. Then it pushes its victim into its mouth, which is suspended from its stomach at the end of a dangling tube.

Is a sea wasp an insect?

The sea wasp is a jellyfish that gets its name because of its deadly sting. Its sting can be more painful than a wasp's and as dangerous as a poisonous snake's bite.

What's a Portuguese man-of-war?

The Portuguese man-of-war is different from other jellyfish because it is a *colonial* jellyfish. That means it is made up of hundreds of individual jellyfish that work together as one animal. Some are in charge of getting food, others do the swimming, and still others take care of reproduction. The man-of-war has a blue float that sticks above the water's surface. This float is used as a sail—letting the wind move it along.

Amazing *but* TRUE

When a sea slug captures and eats a jellyfish, the jellyfish's poisonous stingers move onto the sea slug's tentacles and provide the slug with protection.

29

Are sea anemones flowers?

Sea anemones look like spectacular underwater flowers. But anyone lured by their beauty soon finds out the truth about them. Anemones are animals, and dangerous ones at that! What look like gracefully swaying petals are really wriggling poisonous tentacles. Each tentacle has hundreds of stingers that shoot a paralyzing poison into any creature that touches them.

Tell Me More

Some anemones have a kind of glue on their tentacles that helps them catch small fish.

Here come the clowns

Most fish know better than to approach the anemone, but the beautiful orange-and-gold clown fish is an exception. It swims freely among the anemone's tentacles with no fear of being hurt. In fact, as long as the clown fish takes refuge in the anemone, no enemy would dare come near it. The clown fish feeds on scraps of fish and shrimp left over from the anemone's meal.

Even though it is an animal, the jellylike sea anemone has no eyes or brain.

Tell Me More

Though you have come to the last page of this book, you are only beginning to know about the wonderful true-life stories of fish. Scientists who study fish are called *ichthyologists*. But you don't have to be an ichthyologist to enjoy finding out more about these amazing members of the animal kingdom.

There seems to be a plan and a purpose for everything in nature. Large or small, beautiful or strange, each plant and animal has a role to fulfill. Each has an effect on something else that sooner or later has an effect on us.

Here are some more amazing-but-true facts to start you on your way to new discoveries:

- The archerfish shoots insects out of the air with a spurt of water that works like a water gun.

- Puffer fish inflate their bodies with water so they become too big to be swallowed.

- Coelacanths, fish that lived in the days of the dinosaurs—seventy million years ago—still exist today near the island of Madagascar.

- When water is polluted, fish suffocate because they can't get oxygen from the water.

- Lungfish have both lungs and gills. When their water homes dry up during the dry season, they build themselves a mud cocoon and sleep until summer is over.

- Salmon live in the ocean, but return to lay their eggs in the freshwater rivers where they were born. They find their way back because they remember the smell of their birthplace.